Francis Frith's

BEDFORDSHIRE
LIVING MEMORIES

photographs of the mid twentieth century

Francis Frith's

BEDFORDSHIRE
LIVING MEMORIES

Derryck Draper

First published in the United Kingdom in 2002 by
The Francis Frith Collection

Hardback Edition 2002
ISBN 1-85937-513-8

Paperback edition 1-84589-251-8
Text and Design copyright The Francis Frith Collection®
Photographs copyright The Francis Frith Collection®
except where indicated.

The Frith® photographs and the Frith® logo are reproduced under licence from
Heritage Photographic Resources Ltd, the owners of the Frith® archive and trademarks.
'The Francis Frith Collection', 'Francis Frith' and 'Frith' are registered trademarks of
Heritage Photographic Resources Ltd.

British Library Cataloguing in Publication Data

Bedfordshire Living Memories
Derryck Draper

The Francis Frith Collection
Frith's Barn, Teffont,
Salisbury, Wiltshire SP3 5QP
Tel: +44 (0) 1722 716 376
Email: info@francisfrith.co.uk
www.francisfrith.co.uk

Printed and bound in Great Britain

Front Cover: BIGGLESWADE, Market Place c1955 B93049t
The colour-tinting is for illustrative purposes only, and is not intended to be historically accurate

AS WITH ANY HISTORICAL DATABASE THE FRITH ARCHIVE IS CONSTANTLY BEING CORRECTED AND IMPROVED
AND THE PUBLISHERS WOULD WELCOME INFORMATION ON OMISSIONS OR INACCURACIES

contents

Francis Frith: Victorian Pioneer

FRANCIS FRITH, Victorian founder of the world-famous photographic archive, was a complex and multi-talented man. A devout Quaker and a highly successful Victorian businessman, he was both philosophic by nature and pioneering in outlook.

By 1855 Francis Frith had already established a wholesale grocery business in Liverpool, and sold it for the astonishing sum of £200,000, which is the equivalent today of over £15,000,000. Now a multi-millionaire, he was able to indulge his passion for travel. As a child he had pored over travel books written by early explorers, and his fancy and imagination had been stirred by family holidays to the sublime mountain regions of Wales and Scotland. 'What a land of spirit-stirring and enriching scenes and places!' he had written. He was to return to these scenes of grandeur in later years to 'recapture the thousands of vivid and tender memories', but with a different purpose. Now in his thirties, and captivated by the new science of photography, Frith set out on a series of pioneering journeys to the Nile regions that occupied him from 1856 until 1860.

Intrigue and Adventure

He took with him on his travels a specially-designed wicker carriage that acted as both dark-room and sleeping chamber. These far-flung journeys were packed with intrigue and adventure. In his life story, written when he was sixty-three, Frith tells of being held captive by bandits, and of fighting 'an awful midnight battle to the very point of surrender with a deadly pack of hungry, wild dogs'. Sporting flowing Arab costume, Frith arrived at Akaba by camel seventy years before Lawrence, where he encountered 'desert princes and rival sheikhs, blazing with jewel-hilted swords'.

During these extraordinary adventures he was assiduously exploring the desert regions bordering the Nile and patiently recording the antiquities and peoples with his camera. He was the first photographer to venture beyond the sixth cataract. Africa was still the mysterious 'Dark Continent', and Stanley and Livingstone's historic meeting was a decade into the future. The conditions for picture taking confound belief. He laboured for hours in his wicker dark-room in the sweltering heat of the desert, while the volatile chemicals fizzed dangerously in their trays. Often he was forced to work in remote tombs and caves where conditions were cooler. Back in London he exhibited his photographs and was 'rapturously cheered' by members of the Royal Society. His reputation as a photographer was made overnight. An eminent modern historian has likened their impact on the population of the time to that on our own generation of the first photographs taken on the surface of the moon.

Venture of a Life-Time

Characteristically, Frith quickly spotted the opportunity to create a new business as a specialist publisher of photographs. He lived in an era of immense and sometimes violent change. For the poor in the early part of Victoria's reign work was a drudge and the hours long, and people had precious little free time to enjoy themselves. Most had no transport other than a cart or gig at their disposal, and had not travelled far beyond the boundaries of their own town or village. However,

by the 1870s, the railways had threaded their way across the country, and Bank Holidays and half-day Saturdays had been made obligatory by Act of Parliament. All of a sudden the ordinary working man and his family were able to enjoy days out and see a little more of the world.

With characteristic business acumen, Francis Frith foresaw that these new tourists would enjoy having souvenirs to commemorate their days out. In 1860 he married Mary Ann Rosling and set out with the intention of photographing every city, town and village in Britain. For the next thirty years he travelled the country by train and by pony and trap, producing fine photographs of seaside resorts and beauty spots that were keenly bought by millions of Victorians. These prints were painstakingly pasted into family albums and pored over during the dark nights of winter, rekindling precious memories of summer excursions.

The Rise of Frith & Co

Frith's studio was soon supplying retail shops all over the country. To meet the demand he gathered about him a small team of photographers, and published the work of independent artist-photographers of the calibre of Roger Fenton and Francis Bedford. In order to gain some understanding of the scale of Frith's business one only has to look at the catalogue issued by Frith & Co in 1886: it runs to some 670 pages, listing not only many thousands of views of the British Isles but also many photographs of most European countries, and China, Japan, the USA and Canada – note the sample page shown on page 9 from the hand-written *Frith & Co* ledgers detailing pictures taken. By 1890 Frith had created the greatest specialist photographic publishing company in the

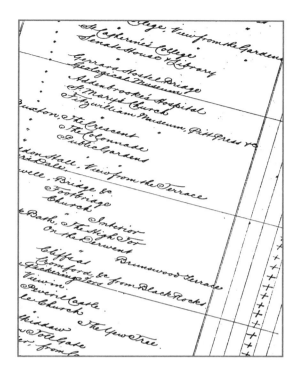

a year after Frith's death, a new card measuring 5.5 x 3.5 inches became the standard format, but it was not until 1902 that the divided back came into being, with address and message on one face and a full-size illustration on the other. *Frith & Co* were in the vanguard of postcard development, and Frith's sons Eustace and Cyril continued their father's monumental task, expanding the number of views offered to the public and recording more and more places in Britain, as the coasts and countryside were opened up to mass travel.

Francis Frith died in 1898 at his villa in Cannes, his great project still growing. The archive he created continued in business for another seventy years. By 1970 it contained over a third of a million pictures of 7,000 cities, towns and villages. The massive photographic record Frith has left to us stands as a living monument to a special and very remarkable man.

world, with over 2,000 outlets – more than the combined number that Boots and W H Smith have today! The picture on the right shows the *Frith & Co* display board at Ingleton in the Yorkshire Dales (left of window). Beautifully constructed with a mahogany frame and gilt inserts, it could display up to a dozen local scenes.

Postcard Bonanza

The ever-popular holiday postcard we know today took many years to develop. In 1870 the Post Office issued the first plain cards, with a pre-printed stamp on one face. In 1894 they allowed other publishers' cards to be sent through the mail with an attached adhesive halfpenny stamp. Demand grew rapidly, and in 1895 a new size of postcard was permitted called the court card, but there was little room for illustration. In 1899,

Frith's Archive: A Unique Legacy

FRANCIS FRITH'S legacy to us today is of immense significance and value, for the magnificent archive of evocative photographs he created provides a unique record of change in 7,000 cities, towns and villages throughout Britain over a century and more. Frith and his fellow studio photographers revisited locations many times down the years to update their views, compiling for us an enthralling and colourful pageant of British life and character.

We tend to think of Frith's sepia views of Britain as nostalgic, for most of us use them to conjure up memories of places in our own lives with which we have family associations. It often makes us forget that to Francis Frith they were records of daily life as it was actually being lived in the cities, towns and villages of his day. The Victorian age was one of great and often bewildering change for ordinary people, and though the pictures evoke an impression of slower times, life was as busy and hectic as it is today.

We are fortunate that Frith was a photographer of the people, dedicated to recording the minutiae of everyday life. For it is this sheer wealth of visual data, the painstaking chronicle of changes in dress, transport, street layouts, buildings, housing, engineering and landscape that captivates us so much today. His remarkable images offer us a powerful link with the past and with the lives of our ancestors.

Today's Technology

Computers have now made it possible for Frith's many thousands of images to be accessed almost instantly. In the Frith archive today, each photograph is carefully 'digitised' then stored on a CD Rom. Frith archivists can locate a single photograph amongst thousands within seconds. Views can be catalogued and sorted under a variety of categories of place and content to the immediate benefit of researchers.

Inexpensive reference prints can be created for them at the touch of a mouse button, and a wide range of books and other printed materials assembled and published for a wider, more general readership - in the next twelve months over a hundred Frith local history titles will be published! The day-to-day workings of the archive are very different from how they were in Francis Frith's time: imagine the herculean task of sorting through eleven tons of glass negatives as Frith had to do to locate a particular sequence of pictures!

See Frith at www.francisfrith.co.uk

Yet the archive still prides itself on maintaining the same high standards of excellence laid down by Francis Frith, including the painstaking cataloguing and indexing of every view.

It is curious to reflect on how the internet now allows researchers in America and elsewhere greater instant access to the archive than Frith himself ever enjoyed. Many thousands of individual views can be called up on screen within seconds on one of the Frith internet sites, enabling people living continents away to revisit the streets of their ancestral home town, or view places in Britain where they have enjoyed holidays. Many overseas researchers welcome the chance to view special theme selections, such as transport, sports, costume and ancient monuments.

We are certain that Francis Frith would have heartily approved of these modern developments in imaging techniques, for he himself was always working at the very limits of Victorian photographic technology.

The Value of the Archive Today

Because of the benefits brought by the computer, Frith's images are increasingly studied by social historians, by researchers into genealogy and ancestory, by architects, town planners, and by teachers and schoolchildren involved in local history projects.

In addition, the archive offers every one of us an opportunity to examine the places where we and our families have lived and worked down the years. Highly successful in Frith's own era, the archive is now, a century and more on, entering a new phase of popularity.

The Past in Tune with the Future

Historians consider the Francis Frith Collection to be of prime national importance. It is the only archive of its kind remaining in private ownership and has been valued at a million pounds. However, this figure is now rapidly increasing as digital technology enables more and more people around the world to enjoy its benefits.

Francis Frith's archive is now housed in an historic timber barn in the beautiful village of Teffont in Wiltshire. Its founder would not recognize the archive office as it is today. In place of the many thousands of dusty boxes containing glass plate negatives and an all-pervading odour of photographic chemicals, there are now ranks of computer screens. He would be amazed to watch his images travelling round the world at unimaginable speeds through network and internet lines.

The archive's future is both bright and exciting. Francis Frith, with his unshakeable belief in making photographs available to the greatest number of people, would undoubtedly approve of what is being done today with his lifetime's work. His photographs, depicting our shared past, are now bringing pleasure and enlightenment to millions around the world a century and more after his death.

Bedfordshire - An Introduction

BEDFORDSHIRE - ONE OF ENGLAND'S smaller counties - was my home from the 1930s until the late 1960s, with a diversion or two along the way on behalf of Queen and country and various commercial concerns. As a youngster, most of the county's 300,000 acres were my playground, because the first half of the 20th century saw little development beyond the urban boundaries established prior to the Great War, and there were vast areas of rural space easily accessible to 'a boy and a bike'.

Relatives owned a farm on the edge of the village of Silsoe. Family friends also farmed on part of what is now (in my opinion) the concrete, brick and glass devastation of Milton Keynes. Our family home was located on the then extreme southern edge of Luton, less than a mile from ancient Saxon field systems impressed into the Chiltern Hills, woods carpeted with bluebells in the Spring and hedgerows laden with free produce in the Autumn. The long summer holidays, which occasionally included several days of agricultural 'work', were absolutely wonderful. As in all the best memories, summer rain fell only at night; the snow was crisp and deep in winter; and foggy days were fun.

In the late 1950s demographic pressures, and substantial increases in personal wealth, led to all the major conurbations in the county - Bedford - Luton - Dunstable - Leighton Buzzard - expanding their boundaries in developer-led rapid-build programmes. It is an understatement to say that most of the results were less than ideal and 'estate blight' soon threatened some of the greener parts of Bedfordshire and, latterly, the financial health of the new homeowners. Possibly there was no other answer available at the time, given the size of the problem, but a

little more sensitivity on the part of architects and developers would not have been amiss.

The county is approximately 36 miles north-to-south, 20 miles east-to-west, lumpishly rectangular in shape and encompassed by Buckinghamshire (west), Northamptonshire (north-west), Cambridgeshire (north-east), and Hertfordshire (south-east). Until the application of the 1974 boundary review, the history-laden county of Huntingdonshire occupied the north-eastern quadrant.

With land regularly refreshed by the waters of the Great Ouse and its tributary the Ivel, central and north Bedfordshire is fertile in the extreme and has been a stronghold of market gardening and farming for centuries. From Bartholomew's Gazetteer of the British Isles, 1887: 'The country along the banks of the Ouse and other streams is highly verdant and luxuriant. The greater part of the surface is under tillage; indeed, agriculture, it is said, is further advanced here than in any other English county. On the heavy soils the principal crops are wheat and beans. The sandy and chalky soils of the middle districts are well adapted for horticultural husbandry, and vegetables are extensively grown for the markets of London, Cambridge, &c. There is excellent grazing ground in the SE, this county being noted for its breeds of sheep and cattle. The principal manufactures are agricultural implements and straw-plait for hats.'

The A5, the A6/600 and the A1 trunk roads traverse the county. The original routes were forged as connected elements of long distance trading trails, ridge-bound and linked to a network of byways to give access to adjoining hamlets and villages. Watling Street, Ermine Street and the Icknield Way: the very names lend a romanticism that can never be linked to the M1 motorway. In medieval times, although there was no direct road linking Bedfordshire's county town to the capital city, one direct trade route, possibly a wool road, linked Cambridge, Bedford, Gloucester and Bristol. Technically that route still exists and it is possible to trace it out of Bedford westwards along the A422, north of Milton Keynes, across to Buckingham - Chipping Norton - Stow-on-the-Wold - Gloucester - and then down the Roman road (A38) to Bristol.

Bedford is slightly north of the exact centre of the county, but its positioning in relation to roads and waterways continues to ensure its importance as a place of affairs. Citizens from every location in Bedfordshire continue to acknowledge the town's importance and influence on their lives - regardless of the wishes and, sometimes apparently paranoid, desires of politicians - to move the emphasis elsewhere. In compiling my narrative I too shall use John Bunyan's town as the hub of my journey and, to paraphrase the words of my County, School and Regimental hymn, make good my right to be a Pilgrim.

Bedford from the Air 1959 AFR36079

**Bedford, Town Bridge
c1960** B51054

Bedford Town - The Hub

A document of 880 records the existence of Bedan's ford on the edge of the Fen country. In 1166 Bedford was awarded Borough status by Royal Charter, acknowledging its role as a centre of importance. This was by virtue of its position astride the navigable length of the Great Ouse, at the confluence of the roads that were, seven hundred and fifty years later, to become the A6, the A600 and the A428. The Town Bridge has long since superseded the original ford, and the last guardian of the old trackway was a Norman castle, destroyed in 1224 as the result of a siege by Henry III's forces against Fawkes de Breauté. All that remains of the building is the mound rising from behind the Bedford Museum in Castle Street and the unconsciously commemorative Castle Close on the north bank of the river. ▶

Bedford, Town Bridge c1955 B51143
The significance of Town Bridge is that of an enduring physical presence. In one form or another it has stood on the site for centuries; it carries the main road from the south; it is a symbol of the involvement by the town's citizens with their river. Murkett Brothers car showrooms on the opposite bank in the 1955 picture indicate an unlikely egalitarianism in the juxtaposition of window signs for both Rolls Royce and a caravan agency. By the 1960s the scene had lightened thanks to a coat of paint on the buildings and street furniture, although this photograph was possibly taken early in the year and before the pleasure boat concession had opened for business.

The central positioning of local government administration within the physical county has become one of increasing importance. Despite the 20th-century rise in local economic input from the artificial city of Milton Keynes, some 15 miles to the west, Bedford has lost nothing to the upstart and gained much. Some 1100 years of recorded history, starting with Beda and his ford, has seen to that.

The adjustments to local government boundaries in 1974 brought the village of Kempston into an extended municipal borough. The succeeding years have not been kind to what was, anecdotally, the longest village in England, and which is now a hotchpotch of industrial estates, inadequate infrastructure and every apparent example of bad planning. Far better to stick to the more select environs of Bedford town centre: it has at least retained its market town atmosphere without losing any of the advantages of existence in a modern world.

Bedford, Town Bridge c1960 B51090
A summer picture showing an image that characterises Bedford in the middle of the 20th century as bridge, river and church link under a summer sky. It is close to Regatta Week - as indicated by the decorative 'shields' suspended from the middle piers of the bridge - and probably early on a Sunday morning to judge by the lack of traffic on either the water or the bridge.

Bedford, River Ouse and Town Bridge c1955 B51032

Bedford, View from Town Bridge c1955 B51040
Looking up-river - B51032 - and down-river - B51040 on the Great Ouse, we see scenes far more tranquil than when Danish raiders or Norman soldiery played out their roles. A modern hotel now occupies the area at the southern (left hand) end of the bridge in B51032.

Bedford
The River and Town Bridge c1960 B51086
The 1960s were a decade of great change in Bedford's skyline.
The Swan Hotel acquired a multi-level car park to the rear (its
first concession to the age of the motor car) and the erstwhile car
showrooms at the northern end of Town Bridge were demolished
and replaced with an office block and small retail outlets. In the far
distance one can see the rooftops of modern housing estates built
to accommodate incomers working for new industry in the town.

◄ **Bedford, The Suspension Bridge and Embankment Gardens c1960** B51103
The town's Parks and Gardens department is justifiably proud of its long record of good husbandry in the Embankment Gardens. This display and the repetition of the motto on the side of the bridge was obviously in celebration of a local event in the early 1960s. Although there are no records of what that might have been, the words 'Villa Bedfordia' - Bedford Town - suggest it was as much an outpouring of civic pride in the town itself.

**Bedford, The Great
Ouse and the
Suspension Bridge
c1955** B51144 & B51030
Several months separate
these two views of one
of Bedford's landmarks.
Compare the growth on
the trees and ground
cover - and the quality of
the light on the water.

**Bedford, Embankment
Gardens c1955** B51031
These views of the
Embankment Gardens
clearly show the results
of continuing care and
attention. The town's
War Memorial reminds
of the sacrifices of World
Wars I and II, and the
Korean War. The names
of the dead are not
shown on the memorial,
but are inscribed on
rolls held in the Borough
archives.

Bedford, Castle Close c1960 B51085

Even as a former resident, the author had some trouble locating this view. Castle Close, but not the delightful garden, was incorporated into a major redevelopment of the original location for Bedford Castle. The garden is believed to be now part of Castle Road that runs approximately parallel to the wall on the right of the photograph.

Bedford, Newnham Outdoor Pool c1960 B51081

A very few years after this photograph was taken, the popular Newnham Pool was closed and its place in the leisure activity role taken by a modern facility dedicated to the philanthropy of the Robinson family. The Robinsons were major employers in the town, owing the success of their business activities to the burgeoning TV rental market of the post-war years. Newnham Pool was a good amenity in its day, but its use was severely restricted by the climate, and the decision was taken to build an indoor pool as soon as funds became available.

Bedford
High Street c1955 B51139b

The statue of John Howard, the founder of the Howard League for Penal Reform, broods over the Square - and perhaps over the irony of its location - close to the old Town Gaol that allegedly once held fellow preacher John Bunyan.

Many of the company names on the shop fronts live on in other contexts after nearly half a century. Wells furnishers were related to the brewing family of the same name; the Green Chair sign over the shop intended as a hark back to the craftsman guilds of medieval times. The National Provincial bank is now part of NatWest Bank, itself owned by the Royal Bank of Scotland. The Jaeger Shop on the extreme left of the picture conjures up memories of tweeds and country pursuits; nowadays the brand is much more fashion-orientated, but nevertheless to be found on the High Street in most large market towns. Currys, at the far end of the street, has now moved out of town and operates from a retail park, in common with most of its fellow brand-holders in the DSG Group. The Norvic shoe sign on the right indicates a footwear retailer that specialised in children's styles and fitting. The High Street is now a one-way traffic flow to cope with the influx of daily traffic. For the same reason, it is unlikely that drivers will ever again enjoy the same freedom to park at the side of the road as those in our picture.

Bedford, Bunyan Memorial and Church Green c1955 B51023
Undoubtedly Bedford's most famous son - if only because of his imprisonment as the result of religious intolerance - John Bunyan was born into a tinker's family and lived something of the high life before becoming a Nonconformist preacher. In 1660 he was arrested for his beliefs and spent the next 12 years in prison. Released in 1672, when King Charles II issued the Declaration of Religious Indulgence, he was later returned to gaol when the Declaration was rescinded. The significant and most famous outcome of Bunyan's hardships was the writing and publication, on 18th February 1677, of a religious parable - 'The Pilgrim's Progress'. It became one of the most successful books ever written, being published in over 200 languages. Historical theory has it that it is possible to link Pilgrim's journeying to various locations within Bedfordshire, and the recent establishment of the 'John Bunyan Trail' attempts to add substance to the possibility.

Bedford, St Peter's Square c1960 B51116a
At the opposite end of the High Street from Town Bridge, John Bunyan's statue complements that of John Howard in the Market Place. At least this ensures that Bedford's citizens are never far from reminders of 'fire and brimstone' sermons and exhortations to live exemplary lives.

Bedford, Bedford School c1950 B51003
Bedford School celebrated 450 years of independent education in 2002. Endowed by both the Harpur Trust and the Bedford School Trust, the former owns the school - and three others in Bedford - and the latter exists to hold certain funds and property for its general benefit.

Bedford, Bedford School c1955 B51139f
Sir William Harpur, a local merchant who subsequently became Lord Mayor of London, established the Harpur Trust in 1556 as an educational endowment. The Bedford School Trust was established in 1926 and has been developed into a valuable source of funding, which is not dependent on fee income, for the School and those connected with it. Money is made available for a variety of purposes including building projects and the annual award of a number of scholarships.

Kempston
The Barracks c1955 K96001

The Regimental Depot of the 16th Foot, the Bedfordshire Regiment, Kempston Barracks was opened in 1876 and the first members of the Regiment arrived in May 1877. In 1918 it was designated as the Regimental Headquarters of the Bedfordshire & Hertfordshire Regiment. During World War II the barracks was primarily a convalescent unit.

Kempston Barracks closed in 1958 and stood redundant for many years, although its fives courts were in use as a leisure facility at least until 1969. More recently the site has been given a new lease of life as a Masonic lodge, although part of the original Barracks, including the Keep, is to remain as a link to the Regimental War Memorial sited on the opposite side of Bedford Road.

On a personal note, it was at Kempston Barracks in the late 1920s that the author's father enlisted into the King's Company, Grenadier Guards. Several years later, his son was to follow down a similar road, although that particular journey started in St Albans and finished in Kempston.

Kempston
The War Memorial c1955 K96004

Commemorating those serving members of the Bedfordshire and
Hertfordshire Regiment who gave their lives during World Wars I and
II, and from 1945 to 1958, the Memorial consists of a small rotunda
fronted by two pillars and a small garden of remembrance to the rear.
The ashes of the men killed since 1945 are scattered in the garden.
On 11th November 1950, a particularly raw autumn day, HM Queen
Elizabeth (late the Queen Mother) unveiled the Book of Remembrance
listing over 1,000 men of the regiment killed during the World War II.
She was attended by an honour guard consisting of units drawn from
the regular Regiment, the Territorial Army and the Bedfordshire and
Hertfordshire affiliated units of the Combined and Army Cadet Force.

Kempston, The High Street and Memorial c1955 K96006

Kempston, The Cross Roads c1955 K96007

These photographs depict areas that are less than a hundred yards apart; it is unlikely that the tranquillity portrayed was ever seen after 1960. The centre of Kempston has undergone such a transformation that it is almost impossible to identify the locations of the majority of the buildings shown, and the inclusion of a massive industrial estate into the local development plan has meant that all the roads have been widened to cater for an appropriate increase in heavy commercial traffic. In the late 1960s the Carpenter's Arms on the left of K96007 was owned by the Rogers family, whose son 'Budge' was a stalwart of the Bedford Rugby club and the national team. Following a severe injury he was for many years a selector for the England RFU.

◀ **Kempston, The Mill c1960** K96014
In the early 1970s the mill was a definite 'No Go' area for Kempston children. Semi-derelict; a collection of rusting iron and crumbling brick, its former glories (few) were well hidden. The mill was originally water-driven and it is believed to have been converted to steam power in the early part of the 20th century in an effort to stay viable. The slipway indicates that the river was the main transportation method, barges bringing in grain from the northern and eastern wheat-growing areas and removing the flour to merchants' storage in Bedford.

◄ **Kempston, All Saints' Church c1955** K96012
Standing on the bank of the Great Ouse
about a mile from the centre of Kempston,
the parish church is a stone building wherein
the tower, at least, is Norman in origin. The
belfry contains six bells, two of which are said
to have been cast in 1603 and 1619.
In the manner of a number of older village
churches, All Saints' stands clear of the
original village and incomers find this rather
puzzling, that is until the river floods in
winter. Then the building stands clear of the
waters, but the roads leading to it can be
immersed for several days at a time.

▼ **Kempston, The River
c1965** K96302

◄ **Kempston
Boating on the River
c1965** K96303
The Great Ouse is
as much a part of
Kempston life as it is
that of Bedford. The
water meadows used to
be easily accessible, but
there is little doubt that
modern 'social policing'
will have removed
the spontaneity from
the boating activities
shown in these two
photographs.

Turvey, The Three Cranes Hotel c1950 T90007
Originally known as 'The Chequers', the building style established by the Higgins family is strongly evident in the hotel. Note the old Cyclists Touring Club seal of approval carried above the front entrance - the author has strong memories of excellent sandwiches and good ale. Birds figure strongly in the coats of arms for many landed Bedfordshire families, and it is likely that the cranes of the hotel's sign were borrowed from one of them.

Turvey, Turvey House and the Great Ouse c1955 T90025b
The view across the water meadows is undoubtedly the best aspect for John Higgins' erstwhile home. It takes but a little imagination to people the parkland with yeoman and gentry; ladies in muslins 'enduring' the heat of a summer's day and children floating rudimentary craft on the water while dipping their toes.

North West to Turvey and Harold

Running north-west to Northampton and then on to Coventry, the A428 serves as the main artery for the fertile lands and farms of the Great Ouse valley. Motorists who dislike motorways, and can read a map, use it as an escape route from the M1. Turvey is roughly halfway between Bedford and Northampton and is famous for two attributes: lacemaking and the Abbey. Both are eccentrically British as claims to fame. Lace making is no longer practised by other than a few devotees, but the nuns of the Benedictine Order at Turvey Abbey devote much of their time to handwork beautiful religious embroidery and vestments.

In 1786, however, Abbey Farm (now known as Turvey Abbey) was occupied by Charles Higgins Esq, after his purchase of the estates of the Mordaunt family. The building had never been an abbey, but took its name from the lands owned by the Benedictine Abbey of Bec in Normandy. Two centuries later, in 1981, the Higgins heir of that time invited an order of Benedictine nuns to take residence - a situation that prevails today.

Charles Higgins sold a substantial part of his holdings to his cousin John, who built Turvey House in 1794. Together, the cousins rebuilt much of Turvey in the style we see today and established architectural mores that have been adopted as the modern standard for the village.

Harrold has become commuter territory, with substantial residential development eating into

◀ **Harrold, The Pound and Thatched Cottage c1960** H261005
Although the base of the building may be older, the village lock-up was certainly in use during Victorian times. Harroldians are particularly protective of their heritage. As a teenager the author once parked his 'cycle against the walls as he attempted to look inside, and received a sound telling-off from a resident for 'damaging they walls'.

the prettier areas surrounding the original village. Fortunately the heart, with its 18th-century market house and the village pound - or lock-up - retains its rural character. The development of the Harrold-Odell (pronounced 'odl'), Country Park, on land reclaimed from sand and gravel excavations, has added to the popularity of the area.

Harrold
The Green and Butter Market c1960
H261021a

Generally known as 'The Market House', the building is 18th century in origin and formed a covered area wherein farmers wives and younger members of their families could display dairy products and similar perishables. A relative of the author once divulged that it should have been called 'The Gossip House', for obvious reasons.

Harrold
The Bridge c1960 H261021d

Not a usual view of the old bridge over the Great Ouse, but a good one to study the argument of style against practicality. Built to carry farm and village traffic, it has endured successive modification to bring it to a 20th-century specification. Fortunately this has been achieved with little visible adjustment of the original brick and stonework.

South West to Leighton Buzzard

Despite having diverse characters and a beautiful simplicity in style, the villages and towns in the west of Bedfordshire have lost much to the encroaching development by their economically stronger neighbour, Milton Keynes. Fortunately, individuals and local special interest societies have also preserved a great deal, keeping the worst depredations at bay. Main access roads have been routed away from village centres and the design character of the new housing stock has been forced into conformity with the best elements of the existing homes - many of which date back to the 18th century.

Once the most gentle of beginnings for a morning drive, the twenty-five miles to the Vauxhall Motors plant in Luton - the Kempston to Aspley Guise road - is now a grinding drag, populated day and night with heavy commercial traffic. Industrial estates built at Kempston and on the sites of the brickworks at Stewartby and Marston Moretaine disgorge trucks heading for Junction 11 on the M1 motorway. Delivery vehicles on the reverse run add to the chaos.

The author counts himself fortunate that he knew this road when it was little more than a country byway, when a double puncture merely meant a safe walk the couple of miles to the next garage - something one would not even consider now.

Aspley Guise, The Square c1955 A161014
The grocery store on the right of the picture was part of a small chain that specialised in rural community operation and catered for 'discerning' customers. The personal nature of the other stores indicated that the owners were committed to a high level of involvement in local affairs. The motor car in the centre of the picture is a Jowett Javelin - arguably one of the very best vehicles designed in post-war Britain. The Javelin ceased production in 1953 on the demise of the manufacturing company.

Aspley Guise, Bedford Road c1955 A161009
These delightful properties were an indication of the quality of life in the village in the 1950s. The building on the left appears to have been ancillary to the larger building - possibly a bailiff's tied cottage at some time or other.

Woburn, High Street c1955 W300001
Early Woburn suffered by fire in 1505, and again in 1724, but was entirely rebuilt on both occasions. The second time it was rebuilt with the benevolent assistance of the Duke of Bedford, a fact that is reflected in the open aspect of its modern layout and the quality of the Georgian facades on the main road through the village.

Woburn
Bedford Street c1955 W300005
The date on this photograph is the year in which the Duke of Bedford opened
Woburn Abbey to visitors in the truly commercial sense. There is little in the
picture to indicate that the town was about to enter an era of prosperity as a
'honey pot' tourist trap, although there can be no doubt that the genteel 'tea
rooms' on the right will rapidly have been inundated as the visitor numbers rose.
The grounds of Woburn Abbey were officially 'out of bounds' prior to 1955, but
nevertheless gave an excellent grounding in country lore to teenagers who were
allowed to believe that they were outwitting the estate staff - just as long as no
damage was caused in the process. Just out of picture, on the left, are the buildings
of the village school originally established by Francis, the 5th Earl of Bedford.

◄ **Leighton Buzzard, All Saints' Church c1965** L211013
Leighton Buzzard's name has nothing directly to do with birds of prey, despite several local organisations adopting the title 'The Buzzards' and using the hawk as an emblem. Leighton is a corruption of the Old English for a leek (or vegetable) farm, and Buzzard is an extension of the family name of Theobald de Busar, the first prebendary for the area. The architecture of the parish church suggests a 13th-century influence and the 190ft spire dominates the roofline on all the approaches to the town. This is the second ecclesiastical building to stand on the site.

◄ **Woburn Abbey
The Park c1960**
W301037
The opening of Woburn
Abbey to the general
public introduced many
to the delights of a rural
involvement without
the necessity to move
home and hearth. It
was many years later
that the enjoyment
given by proximity to
the native deer led to
the establishment of the
safari park as a major
part of the attraction of a
day out at Woburn.
In the mid-1960s the
Bedfordshire branch
of the Sporting Owner
Drivers Club (SODC
- known as The Sods)
used a steep hill not too
far from the location
of this picture as the
regular venue for a series
of hill-climbing events.

◄ **Leighton Buzzard, High Street
c1965** L211050
The High Street supports a
busy market on Tuesdays and
Saturdays, but this picture gives
some indication of the potential
for conflict of interests as
traffic volume increases. Some
improvement work has already
been carried out (compare this
photograph with L211032 pages
40-41) and the main buildings are
being renovated in preparation for
a hopefully prosperous future.
Many of the shop fascias carry local
names, a situation that possibly
prevails today as major chains
move to out-of-town centres and
purpose-built premises.

Leighton Buzzard Market Day c1955

L211032

A large number of the buildings in the picture are now Grade II listed, but it is not likely that the unkempt state of the High Street in 1955 did much to foster civic pride. In the 21st century the area has, for some years, been partially pedestrianised and a bypass built to take the ever-increasing volume of traffic.

Leighton Buzzard, The Canal and Globe Inn c1955 L211089
There has been a hostelry on this site for many centuries, but this version was originally built to cater for the navigators who built the Grand Union Canal. Later it welcomed the men and women who plied their trade on the waters. Now its clientele are weekenders, fishermen and leisure sailors.

Linslade, The Grand Union Canal c1960 L212002
The coming of firstly the Grand Union Canal and then the railways, led to the establishment of modern Linslade at its present location. The place name dates back to the 11th century, but the original village fell into disuse and no trace of it remains today. Until 1966, Linslade was a small, mainly Victorian town located in Buckinghamshire. Local government boundary changes brought Leighton Buzzard and Linslade together into the town of Leighton-Linslade and placed them both in Bedfordshire. The River Ouzel - the original boundary between the counties - divides the jointly-named town.

Around Ampthill

Running along the eastern edge of the old brickfields, the A418 and A5120 provide a fast link between the county town and mid-Bedfordshire. With the exception of the northern section, development has been restricted by virtue of the large amount of publicly-owned land that borders it. General Motors established a vehicle proving ground at Millbrook in the 1970s, using the site of a military small-arms range that had been in regular use for almost eighty years.

On the other side of the A418, Houghton House stands on a small hill facing Ampthill. Built between 1615 and 1621 by Lady Pembroke, sister of Sir Philip Sydney, the building is reputedly the 'House Beautiful' of Bunyan's 'The Pilgrim's Progress'.

Ampthill
The Woods c1955 A158002

This cluster of sparse conifers in Ampthill Park borders an entrance to the Cheshire Home for the Disabled that occupies a house built in 1686-88 for the Dowager Countess of Ailesbury and Elgin. Ampthill Park was for many years the venue for large bi-annual camps organised by the Scout Movement in Bedfordshire.

The first settlement in this central valley was 'Aemethyll' in Old English, which translates to 'ant-heap' or 'ant-infested hill'. As one who has camped in Ampthill Park, the writer can vouch for the accuracy of the name. King Henry VIII and his court paid many visits to Ampthill Castle, including a final journey in which he brought his first wife, Katherine of Aragon, to Ampthill for the last years of their married life.

The marriage was annulled in 1533 and Katherine was proclaimed Princess Dowager. The Castle no longer exists, but Katherine's Cross stands in Ampthill Park as a memorial to the tragic event.

▼ **Ampthill, Market Place c1955** A158013

King Henry III gave a charter to the town in 1219, and renewed it in 1242, confirming the right to hold a market on Thursdays. The practise prevails into the 21st century, although the site has moved from the Market Place to the car park of a local supermarket. The bunting and flags visible in this photograph suggest that it might have been taken in Coronation Year, 1953.

▼ **Ampthill, Market Place c1960** A158070

All the main roads converge here, and Ampthill's history as a coaching stop is still visible in the form of the White Hart Hotel on the right of this picture. Much of the building is of Tudor origin, but later additions are said to include panelling removed from Houghton House. The Market Place has been redeveloped at the end of the last century as a Millennium project.

▲ **Ampthill, Church Street c1955** A158019

◀ **Ampthill, Church Street c1965** A158067
Characterised by widely divergent architectural styles, some of the buildings on this street date back to the 16th century. Shop fascias show a wide mixture of businesses serving the community in the 1960s. The majority were owned and operated by local people.

**Ampthill, Woburn Street ▶
c1965** A158080

**Ampthill, Woburn Street ▼
c1955** A158032

These two photographs are reverse views, taken ten years apart. The pub sign showing the Queen's Head refers to Katherine of Aragon. In common with most hostelries in mid-Bedfordshire, the owning brewery is a local to the county, in this case Charles Wells of Bedford. Flowers Brewery, on the opposite side of the road, was based in Luton, having bought out the J W Green's concern some years previously.

◄ **Ampthill, Woburn Street c1965** A158051
Dating back to the 18th century, the deed to each of these cottages restricts the householder to replacing the roof only with thatch, and further prescribes the method and colour of redecoration that may be carried out. It is doubtful that the legality of the covenant has ever been challenged because none of the owners known to the writer have ever wished to change the exteriors of their homes.

Ampthill, St Andrew's Church c1965 (above) A158071 and **Ampthill, The Almshouses c1955** (below) A158012
A number of sources quote Ampthill's parish church as being 10th century, without offering a precise dating.
It is entirely possible that Katherine of Aragon worshipped here during her stay at Ampthill Castle.
Inside the church there is a marble memorial to the life of Colonel Richard Nicolls, who captured the Dutch
Colonial city of New Amsterdam on behalf of the English Crown - and then renamed it New York in honour
of his commanding officer, James, Duke of York. The memorial carries a cannon ball in its base, said to be the
one that killed Colonel Nicolls during the Battle of Sole Bay in 1672.
The Church Square, including the almshouses, is part of the second largest Conservation Area in Bedfordshire.
Very little has changed visually to St Andrew's church and the almshouses for many centuries, apart from
upgraded lighting and the ramifications of normal maintenance. Some of the almshouses date back to the
15th century and a recent programme of refurbishment and modernisation has been carried out to make
them more comfortable for the residents.

Steppingley
The Village c1955 S380001
Steppingley was for many years one of the prettiest villages
in the county, and can still hold its head high in this regard. It
has two claims to fame. The first is the quality of the food and
ales at the local hostelry - the French Horn in the centre of
the picture - which have assured it an international fan club.
The second is the fact that Steppingley was once owned by
New College, Oxford. The ownership lasted for 50 years in
the 16th century. It is not recorded why the College gave up
its potentially lucrative holding.

Flitton
The Barn, Brook Lane c1955 F107003

Typical of many older cottages in central Bedfordshire, the mixture of timber cladding, wattle and daub, tile and thatch gives The Barn a picture postcard look to be envied. Its location at the entrance to Brook Lane is a mixed blessing. Church and pub are conveniently to hand - literally just around the corner - but Brook Lane is also the walking access to the Flitton Moor nature conservation priority area.

Formerly part of a large, open and periodically flooded area, shared for centuries as common land by Flitton and Maulden parishes, Flitton Moor was used as common rough grazing for sheep, cattle and geese throughout the medieval period and until the 19th century. It was largely undrained and undivided until then, when parliamentary enclosure in Maulden parish resulted in a straight drain being dug across the moor. The land to the north-west went into Maulden parish and the rest went to Flitton parish. The course of the River Flit here was straightened at the beginning of the 19th century and now marks the south-eastern boundary of the site.

Flitton
St John the Baptist Church c1955 F107004
The church was recorded as an 'ancient edifice' at the end of the 19th
century. In common with many similar, the Parish Records date from the
16th century, but the building is patently much older than that.
As a boy I recall hearing a tale concerning gold being found in the village
of Pulloxhill, just to the south of Flitton, and decided to try my luck.
Enquiries of residents proved to be fruitless and so I cycled to Flitton and
cornered the incumbent of the parish church. The vicar advised that gold
had indeed been found - but it was at the beginning of the 18th century
and had come to naught. In retrospect, I am grateful that the vicar took my
request seriously - and comforted my disappointment with a cup of tea.

Flitton, The White Horse c1955 F107008 ▶
Flitton, The White Hart c1955 F107005 ▼

What could be termed the perfect situation: a Charles Wells pub at one end of the High Street and a Wells and Winch pub at the other. The former brewery company is still going strong as the largest family-owned brewer in the UK. The other was sold to Greene King of Bury St Edmunds in 1961. Since Flitton enjoys the benefits of two pubs, with the most common names - The White Hart and The White Horse - it might be of interest to explain that the hart is taken from the coat of arms of King Richard II. The horse is a carry-over from the days when few customers could read and an easily recognisable inn sign was a method of ensuring that potential customers found the right doorway.

▼ **Flitton, High Street c1955** F107009

◄ Flitwick, Church Hill c1955

F108003

The one-time village has become a small town as massive over-development relieved the pressure points of Dunstable, Ampthill and Bedford. As a consequence, the rural nature of the area has disappeared under brick and concrete. The parish church of St Peter and St Paul has a 12th-century base, on to which a widened chancel was added in the 13th century. The bell tower was added a century later.

◄ **Flitwick, The Mill c1960** F108025
The present building was constructed in the 18th century, but on the site of a mill listed in Domesday. It still houses two grinding stones and most of its machinery, but is no longer a working water mill. The flow of the River Flit was powerful enough to operate three wheels: overshot, undershot and breastshot.

◀ **Flitwick, View from the Manor c1955** F108004
Built in the early seventeenth century, with some
extensions made during the 18th and 19th centuries,
Flitwick Manor is now a luxury hotel. The Brooks
family owned the manor for much of the nineteenth
century, and they were responsible for landscaping
the grounds, including the diversion of a branch of
the River Flit to create a carp lake and a leisure area.

▲ **Westoning,
The Church c1960**
W298007

▼ **Westoning,
The Church Interior
c1955** W298014
Dedicated to St Mary
Magdalene, Westoning's
parish church closely
follows other church
architecture in
Bedfordshire villages,
being in the Early English
style with battlements
and buttresses and a
tower surmounted by
a short spire. Although
the register dates from
around 1560, the
beautiful interior owes
much to restoration
carried out in the mid-
1800s. The stained glass
window dates from
that time as a memorial
to the late lord of the
manor and his wife.

Westoning, The Rectory c1955 W298008
In common with so many rural livings, church and the
manor were closely aligned in Westoning. The rectory
is a good example of the type of living enjoyed by a
country parson in the second half of the 19th century.
Westoning Manor was built in 1843 as the residence
of Major John Coventry-Campion JP, and stood on the
site of an earlier mansion house.
In 1969, long after the Campion family had moved
on, the manor was acquired as a centre for MacIntyre
Care, a charity devoted to the continuing education
and care of people with learning disabilities.
Now the charity has also moved on and the manor has
been sold to a development company, with permission
to build executive-style homes.

Westoning, Church Road c1960 (above) W298009 and **Westoning, Church Road c1960** (below) W298010
These views look both ways down the only access road to the manor and the parish church. The ribbon development is typical of the village as a whole, which probably came into being as a group of cottages for agricultural workers. The contrast in building styles (and space) is remarkable, spread as it was over the span of a century. The closer to the church, the larger the houses and the plots on which they stand. These are likely to have been post-World War II infill building.

This sequence of photographs shows a layout that no longer exists. The original road through the village consisted of two sharp, opposing bends, clearly visible in daylight but not so at night. In the early 1980s, after a series of accidents, the highways authority effectively 'smoothed' the way by inserting an extra stretch of road on the northern access. In addition to making life safer for all concerned, drivers and inhabitants alike, it also provided Westoning with an opportunity to improve its image by removing the 'frontier town' look of the centre of the village.

▼ **Westoning, Park Road c1960** W298001

▲ **Westoning, Flitwick Road c1960** W298013

▼ **Westoning, The Bell c1960** W298016

◄ **Westoning
Flitwick Road c1960**
W298003

Toddington
High Street c1955 T160002
A busy scene for Toddington in the 1950s. The reason may
have been an agricultural sale or some similar event, but the
M1 motorway - which now passes close by - and a high level of
residential development, were still some years away. For modern
Toddington this would represent a very quiet day.

Toddington, The Green c1955 (above) T160013 and **Toddington, The Green c1955** (below) T160014
The heart of the old village and a very useful place to idle away a warm day. Subject to individual
investigation, it is reasonably safe to say that none of the properties surrounding the Green are
younger than the 1890s. Styles vary widely and roofing materials range from thatch to pantiles to
slate - how different from the enforced uniformity of the late 20th century.

Clophill, High Street c1955 C326014
The author declares a personal interest in the village because, for many years, an uncle owned the local shoe repair shop on the High Street. It was little more than a corrugated iron shed, with a high counter shielding the workbench, a treadle operated sewing machine, racks of tools and the smell of leather and wax. Without running water, the tea supply was scrounged from neighbouring premises on a daily basis and kept in a tall cream-coloured jug with a piece of cloth over the top. An old coke stove served as central heating appliance and brew maker. To a small boy it was Heaven.
By 1955 both uncle and shop had long gone, but little seems to have changed otherwise.

▲ Clophill, The Green c1955 C326008
▼ Clophill, The Green c1960 C326021

Not large enough for cricket, but providing a shady spot on a summer's day, the Green also serves as a traffic-calming device. Forty years after these photographs were taken most of the tumbledown properties have disappeared (before an authority could 'list' them no doubt) and the Green has a very spruce air, with a spot of infill building and some tidy thatching on the remainder. The Flying Horse pub was the 'local' to the author's uncle and a hotbed of darts, dominoes and village gossip in days gone. Now it belongs to a national chain of branded pub-food outlets and it is entirely probable that there is no room for a dartboard.

▲ **Clophill, Back Street c1955** C326005
◄ **Clophill, Back Street c1955** C326016
Back Street runs parallel to the High Street and provided similar diversions, as well as a useful getaway route for the local poaching fraternity. The Stone Jug is one of the last of the rural alehouses, where a hand pump at one time was considered to be the Devil's engine and the beer was served from an enamelled jug. The sign on the front of the building suggests that at the time of the photograph it was owned by Flowers Breweries, so it is possible that 'civilised' service was accorded to the photographer on his visit.

▼ Luton, The Museum c1955 L117001

This beautiful old mansion house in Luton's Wardown Park houses a wide variety of standing exhibits - and the curators have an extensive programme of temporary events to hold the visitor's interest. One section is devoted to lacemaking in the county and another to Luton's own traditional industry - hat making. The Bedfordshire and Hertfordshire Regimental museum is also housed within the building. In 2001 the museum department received planning permission for a large new extension.

▼ Luton, Town Hall c1960
L117088

At this time controlled by a simple set of three traffic lights, the junction of George Street, Upper George Street (left) Wellington Street (out of picture on the left) and Manchester Street (right) soon required a multi-function system, complete with laning, bollards and the inevitability of total chaos. Majestically rising over it all are Luton's Town Hall and war memorial. In later years, the municipal building was to acquire 'eyebrows' - a set of semi-permanent offices on the roof of the original building, to cope with an ever-increasing multitude of local government officials - including traffic planners.

▼ Luton, Manchester Street c1955 L117003a

As one of four major thoroughfares leading to the Town Centre, and formerly called Tower Hill, Manchester Street's importance was typified by the presence of many privately-owned shops and businesses and the quality of the buildings they occupied. This junction with Gordon Street (on the left of the picture) is one of the boundaries of 'old' Luton. A wider angle would have shown the architectural changes between the 19th and 20th centuries that are clearly visible, even today.

Dunstable, Luton and the South

Having at various times walked, cycled, driven and flown over the short stretch of the A6 between Bedford and Luton, it is safe to say that I know it well. Despite the depredations in the name of progress, it holds a fascination that ensures a return whenever I am in the vicinity.

Quite apart from the locations in the following narrative, it is worth mentioning Wrest Park House Gardens in Silsoe- once the home of the de Grey family. Cranfield University has a campus nearby and the old agricultural college in Wrest Park is now the Silsoe Research Institute and engaged in the pursuit of biological research. The Old George Hotel on High Street, Silsoe, once provided bed and board to Samuel Johnson during his wanderings around England.

Barton-le-Cley can, and does, live up to its name in wet weather. Barton Springs is the local beauty spot and jumping off point for a good stretch of the legs on the Chilterns to the north of Luton.

Luton, Castle Street c1955 L117013a
This is the junction of George Street, Castle Street and Chapel Street - three titles that follow the 19th- century fashion for objective street names. George - after the monarchs; Castle - because that was the road leading to Robert Waudari's castle (Luton was a gift from King Henry VI); Chapel - because the road led to the Wesleyan chapel. The shops to the right show physical evidence of Luton's ability to graft 20th-century fronts onto 19th-century buildings.

◀ **Luton, Vauxhall Motors c1955**
L117048
The fact that it was possible to park on the side of the road without a problem makes this photograph one to be treasured. The building to the left is K Block; it housed the greater part of the marketing and sales functions for the company. Scaffolding on the right indicates that the Bedford van production facility was undergoing an upgrade, and building works immediately beyond the bridge (which also contained part of the van production line) were part of a major expansion of the local infrastructure to accommodate the growing workforce.

◄ **Luton, Vauxhall Motors c1955** L117035
The Vauxhall Iron Works moved to Luton from its London base in 1905. Thereafter it enjoyed some considerable sporting success and built cars for the wealthy and influential. After World War I, however, the necessity to open its products to a wider clientele imposed financial strains that were only alleviated by the purchase of the company by General Motors in 1925. This view shows the side entrance to the company's canteen, capable of feeding over half the workforce (of around 15,000) at any one time. Facilities also included a fully operational theatrical stage, and broadcasting equipment that was often used by the BBC for light entertainment productions requiring an appreciative audience.

▼ **Luton, Vauxhall Motors c1950** L117028
This picture gives some indication of the scale of operations at Vauxhall Motors. The new production facility under construction in the foreground requires the infrastructure of a residential estate to make it viable. The maintenance and building contractors had their own site operations facility, complete with semi-permanent buildings, security and a full communications system. Note how wartime camouflage paint is still visible; it remained so until at least the late 1970s.

◄ **Luton, Luton Hoo c1955** L117040
Originally designed in 1767 by Robert Adam for the 3rd Earl of Bute, this unique country house was reconstructed in 1843 after a fire in which little of the original building was left untouched. The Hoo was subsequently remodelled in 1903 by the diamond entrepreneur Sir Julius Wernher, and housed the Wernher art collection until recent reversals in the family's affairs led to a sale of the property to an international hotel company. An additional claim to fame is the fact that the-then HRH Princess Elizabeth and HRH The Duke of Edinburgh spent part of their honeymoon here in 1947.

▼ **Caddington, All Saints' Church c1960** C324017

Not the best view of Caddington's 12th-century parish church, because the trees hide an unusual diamond-shaped clock face and the elegance of the tower overall. Caddington History Society restored the clock in 1997 and invited Archbishop Runcie to officiate at its unveiling. To the rear of the church, a well-used footpath leads via a bridleway to 'Bluebell' Wood (now a game bird preserve and therefore a 'no go' area). In season the hedgerows can provide a plentiful supply of blackberries, hazel nuts and wild garlic.

▼ **Caddington, The Green c1960** C324012

The village was ripe for development after World War II and these blocks were the result. New residents were drawn from nearby Luton, which even in 1960 was becoming overcrowded. But the Green remains and provides, at the very least, a focal point.

▲ **Caddington, Manor Road c1960** C324019
◄ **Caddington, Heathfield Road c1960**
C324023

These photographs illustrate development
that occurred in the village during the 1950s.
At the time they were taken, the areas had
matured and therefore lost the brashness that
characterised so much residential building in
the early post-war period.

Dunstable
Priory Church c1955 D69012
King Henry I founded an Augustinian priory here in 1131, built a palace
and established a new market town that rapidly became a place of
considerable importance. Regular royal visits and jousting tournaments
added to the attraction of being sited close to the crossroads of the
Watling Street and the Icknield Way. It was at the priory, in the 16th
century, that the annulment of King Henry VIII's marriage to Katherine of
Aragon was pronounced, followed by the dissolution of the priory itself
soon afterwards. Parts of the original priory church, with its fine Norman
nave and magnificent west front, have survived as the town's parish
church - the Priory Church of St Peter.

Dunstable, High Street South c1950 D69002
Forming a boundary with the original Augustinian priory site established by Henry I, the High Street follows the route of the Watling Street ancient trackway. Beyond the vehicles parked on the left, the hint of an open space indicates the existence of the market square (and occasional bus terminus).

Dunstable, High Street North 1967 D69048
This is the follow-on view from D69002, looking north along the A5 - the Watling Street. The prominent white-peaked emblem on the right hand side of the road indicates the location of one the town's remaining coaching inns, the Sugar Loaf Hotel. The square architecture to the right is an example of infill following the demolition of buildings from an earlier era. A cycle shop on the extreme right belonged to Charlie Cole - a most respected and veteran racing cyclist.

Dunstable
Broad Walk c1965
D69056
It must be assumed that the symbolism of the clock design meant something to the developers of this pedestrianised shopping area, but there is nothing on record to tell us what it might be. The temporary pram park outside the supermarket should be contrasted with the prevailing situation at the beginning of the 21st century, where every perambulator is designed for in-car travel - and no mother would leave her baby unattended while she does the shopping.

◀ **Dunstable**
Grove House Gardens
c1960 D69010
As a major civic amenity, these attractive gardens are the source of great pride to Dunstablians. Planners have managed to combine the old with the new and modern buildings like Dunstable Leisure Centre, Dunstable College, the courthouse and the library are grouped around them.

◄ **Dunstable, Queensway Hall c1965** D69044
Dunstable's civic hall was built during the same period as the Broad Walk shopping precinct, but to much more pleasing dimensions and architectural lines. However, the facility was under-used and in 2000 the site was sold to a major supermarket.

▲ **Dunstable, The Downs c1960** D69014
◄ **Dunstable, Totternhoe from the Gliding Club c1960** D69015

The manifestation of the Chiltern Hills to the south west of Dunstable, the Downs represent a major leisure activity area in southern Bedfordshire. The London Gliding Club has been in residence for many years and the National Trust administers and maintains the quality of the summit. Fond memories for many will include orange rolling at Easter, butterfly cataloguing, dirt-track biking down the rougher paths and walking the ridge through to Whipsnade or Eaton Bray.

Eaton Bray, The Village Green c1955 E104012
The Square (the Green) is the site of the village pump, standing exactly as it was left after mains water arrived.
Perhaps the standpipe indicated a lack of faith on the part of villagers. Many years ago, regular markets were
held here and at the end of summer the villagers enjoyed 'The Stattie Fair'.

Eaton Bray, High Street c1955 E104008
Once the site of brickworks, High Street, like much of the rest of Eaton Bray, has now become a dormitory for
commuters to nearby Dunstable and Luton.

Whipsnade Zoo
The Elephant c1955 W299018
Strictly speaking a part of the London Zoo, Whipsnade has for
many years offered a definitive environment for wild animals,
whilst also allowing them to be viewed by visitors (or perhaps it is
the other way around).

By the middle of the 1960s the increase in the size of the local workforce, particularly in the motor industry, led to a demand for reasonably-priced housing within commuting distance. Many local building companies took the opportunity to develop large estates, sites similar to those shown here, on green field sites in the south of the county. It appears that the school in Houghton Regis is already experiencing growing pains by 1965, if we are to judge from the temporary classroom on the left of H263015.

Houghton Regis, County Primary School ▶
c1965 H263015
Houghton Regis, The Estate c1965 H263012 ▼

◄ **Houghton Regis
Tithe Farm Road
c1965** H263017

Around Shefford

Running almost as straight as its near-neighbour, The Great North Road (A1), this Ermine Street byway links Bedford and Hitchin through the least densely populated part of the county. For the first ten miles one only encounters two small villages, and then only a further two or three during the next seven miles. However, for all the sparseness of population, it is safe to say that this sector is one of the most productive in agricultural terms. Well-watered by tributaries of the Great Ouse and the Ivel, the rich land gives high quality crops and dairy products year after year.

Shefford, High Street c1950 S378004
Shefford is a small market town with Royal Charters dating back to the 13th century. It owes its name and its foundation to the five roads that meet in the town and the fact that at this point it was possible to ford the rivers Hit and Flit. Shefford is a corruption of Sheep Ford - possibly the title bestowed by herders as they moved their flocks across the River Ivel at this point to stay ahead of Danish invaders. On the right of the High Street, the building with the ornate stonework is the Catholic Church of St Francis built in 1884. The sacristy was originally the chapel of St George - the first chapel to be built in Bedfordshire after the Reformation. A small statue of St George is mounted to the side of the entrance to the church. At the far end of the street is the parish church of St Michael and All Angels.

Shefford
The Church and War Memorial c1955 S378005
Probably dating back to a chapel-of-ease on the site in the 14th
century, St Michael and All Angels is a striking landmark visible from
most of the town. Built primarily of local sandstone (not the hardest
of materials), a belt-and-braces parish council authorised the use of
facing bricks to repair the top of the tower. There appears to be no
record of when the work was carried out. The church is unusual in
that it does not have a graveyard. This is because it was originally
a daughter church to Campion, a mile or so to the south-west, and
Shefford would have buried its dead there.

Shefford, North Bridge Street c1960 (above) S378020 and **Shefford, South Bridge Street c1965** (below) S378015
Before local government was established, Shefford was fortunate in the action of a 16th-century resident called
Robert Lucas, who left his property for the benefit of the citizens of Shefford. In 1560, the Robert Lucas Trust was
set up to establish and maintain bridges, highways and causeways in Shefford. In 1750 the Trust did build two
new bridges over the Rivers Hit and Flit, and North Bridge Street and South Bridge Street to run between them.
The Porch on North Bridge may have a tumbledown appearance, but it is the local branch of a major bank and
therefore to be deemed secure against all comers.

◀ **Henlow, The Rotunda c1955** H262301
Known to generations of Royal Air Force trainees, the Rotunda has been known to provide shelter from the rain and snow, a useful trysting spot and an easily recognisable landmark for disorientated drivers.

◄ Shefford, The River c1960 S378017

The 19th century saw an increase in local commercial development, which highlighted the necessity for coal to be brought to the area cheaply. A canal from Biggleswade to Shefford was built in 1822 and gave the town the status of an inland port, with a navigable waterway to King's Lynn. Town and canal prospered for some 50 years but, with the advent of the railway, the Ivel Navigation Trust began to incur heavy losses and in 1876 the Trust and its canal were closed. River Ivel Navigation is marked (Disused) on the maps but some aspects are still visible in the town.

◄ Henlow, The Church c1955 H262307

Bedfordshire abounds in churches of this antiquity. The parish church dedicated to St Mary the Virgin has a recorded history from the 12th century, but there are strong indications that the base of the building is considerably older - although this may only have been a small chapel. Quite apart from its spiritual function, the tower of the church has been a first class landmark for RAF pilots in the past - and continues to be so for the instructors and trainees from Henlow Flying Club.

◄ Lower Stondon Henlow Camp Crossroads 1955
L213003

No doubt a useful source of refreshment in its day, the Ritz Café has apparently seen better times by 1955. Royal Air Force Henlow is now a research and communications facility. The crossroads still exist, but are now 'controlled' by a roundabout.

**Arlesey, Post Office
c1965** A160003
Regrettably, this photograph of Arlesey says it all. A classic case of ribbon development, but with no apparent reason for even existing. Still mainly an agricultural economy, there are one or two instances of light engineering at either end of the High Street.

Arlesey, Fairfield Hospital c1960 A160008
Famed throughout Bedfordshire and Hertfordshire as the Three Counties (an excised part of Huntingdon made up the triumvirate), Fairfield was a mental care facility for many years. It closed in 1998, but the old wives' tales about 'Arlesey' or 'Three Counties' are legion.

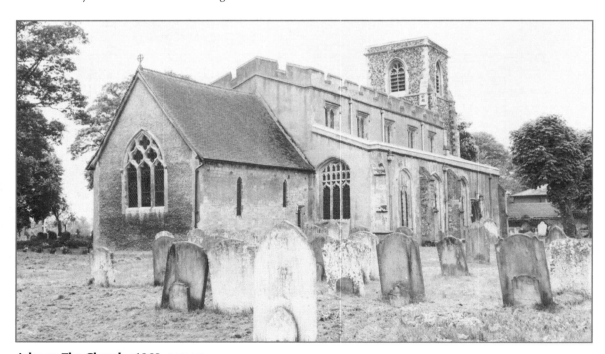

Arlesey, The Church c1960 A160001
Dedicated to St Peter, the parish church stands appropriately at the northern entrance to the village. Originating in the 13th century, the six-bell tower was rebuilt in 1877.

Arlesey
The Blue Lagoon c1960 A160011
It is to be hoped that the photographer sought permission for this shot; if not, then he was trespassing. Despite a widespread belief to the contrary, the Blue Lagoon is a flooded clay pit standing in private grounds and only licensed for restricted use to a few water-based leisure clubs. Nevertheless large numbers of visitors arrive on hot days in summer and this recently gave rise to a tragedy involving prior stupidity with a motor vehicle and the subsequent deaths by drowning of three small children. The driver was jailed for manslaughter.

East to Biggleswade, Sandy and Potton

The short linking route to the A1, the Great North Road, and the market town of Sandy, the A603 passes through Willington and the strangely-named village of Mogerhanger, before erupting into the faster-flowing traffic of the trunk road. Cambridge comes within easy reach by picking up the old Roman road to the east and it is not unlikely that monarchs and princes, clergy and pedants used it to reach the next nearest power centre in Bedford. The Great North Road has history built into every mile - some of it almost believable. Warring tribes, invaders and defenders, non-conformist preachers, rogues and honest men have vested the highway between the capital cities of England and Scotland with romantic legends and true tales. It has caused as many books to be written as there are about the human condition - and they are likely to be much more interesting.

Blunham, The Hill c1965 B295010
Dropping into the Square at the centre of the village, this photograph is taken on the 112ft summit of The Hill. The exit to the right is Station Road, a misnomer since the Beeching axe fell in the 1960s and rendered the old railway station redundant. The egg box architecture on the right of the road has been considerably softened by the passage of time. Current pictures show that many of the homes have been extended and given a level of individuality.

**Blunham, The Hill
and The Square c1965**
B295013
The bottom of The Hill
is also the entrance
to the centre of the
village. The road to
the right is Park Lane,
which provides access
to a section of the
Kingfisher Trail.

Blunham, The Square c1965 B295016
Given nearly a forty-year time lapse, it is not surprising that the shops shown in this picture have now been replaced. The pre-war petrol pump, complete with the Shell globe, is probably in a museum of 20th-century artefacts. The photographer was standing in the High Street; to the right is The Hill.

Blunham, High Street c1965 B295009
This shows the northern entrance to Blunham as a direct access from the Great North Road. Again, the stark nature of the commuter architecture has been softened over the intervening years with many house extensions being built and the maturing of a number of ornamental trees.

Blunham, Footbridge and River Ivel c1965 B295001
This little bridge is at the end of Park Lane and gives access to the Kingfisher Trail that follows the course of the river. In the background is the old rectory, beyond that the parish church.

Blunham, The Church c1965 B295006
St Edmunds is a 12th-century sandstone building in a typical Norman design - although the interior fittings boast a Saxon font as an indication of an earlier place of worship. This is the church to which the preacher and poet John Dunne was appointed Rector in 1621 and remained so until his death in 1631.

▲ **Sandy, From the Sand Hills c1960** S61023
▼ **Sandy, From the Sand Hills c1960** S61028

Sandy is listed in the Domesday Book as Sandeia, possibly derived from the Old English word Sandieg - a sand mound. A promontory known locally as the Sand Hills, from which these fine views were photographed, overlooks the town.

▲ **Sandy, Bedford Road c1955** S61005
As the name of the road suggests, this is the extension of the A603 into the centre of the town. It is doubtful that even on the quietest day this thoroughfare is as traffic-free as in the photograph.

◀ **Sandy, High Street c1960**
S61042
This picture shows the High Street where it passes through the Market Square. At the beginning of the 20th century only a few roads in the town were metalled - High Street being one of them - and any residential and commercial building was confined to ribbon development along them. The rest of the area was given over to market gardening and farming.

Sandy, Market Square 1959 S61021
An early attempt to control parking in the Market Square. Shops were very much of the local variety - most notably the newsagents that sells everything, and a baker and confectioner that looks as though it truly bakes on the premises. The bank appears to be occupying a conversion of one half of a pair of semis.

▼ **Sandy, Potton Road c1955** S61008

As the continuation of the High Street, this road has been subjected to considerable residential pressures since the 1950s. Consequently it is difficult to place this very rural scene in the Sandy of the 21st century. With the ground climbing to the left, it is possible that it is close to the Sand Hills and therefore facing west.

▼ **Sandy, The Mill c1960** S61018

Never a very large town, Sandy owes its continued existence to the strength of the produce market in Victorian England. When the railway came in 1850, it opened up the voracious wholesale markets of London and the Midlands and brought a measure of solid prosperity to the community. This mill was probably one of a number owned by the Jordan family, all bar one of which - in Biggleswade - have ceased production.

▲ **Sutton, Old Packhorse Bridge c1955** S795004

◄ **Sutton, John o' Gaunts Hill c1960** S795372
Packhorse bridges in Bedfordshire are very few and far between. This splendid example demonstrates a subtle irony in the provision of a passing place for those very rare occasions when two animals met en route and the river was in flood. The second photograph (S795072) shows John o' Gaunt's Hill - an ancient monument that has given its name to the local golf club. The packhorse bridge is in the lower left quarter of the picture, hidden by the hedge.

Potton
St Mary's Church c1955 P130002
Originally owing allegiance to the Earldom of Huntingdon,
Potton's parish church owes its architectural features to Norman
influences during the 12th century.

Potton
The Clock House c1955 P130025a
The original clock tower stood on this site in an area known as
The Shambles, closely surrounded by small shops. The new Clock
House was opened in 1955.

**Wrestlingworth
The Village c1960**
W302001
Considered by many
to be idyllic, this quiet
corner of Bedfordshire
has its roots deep in the
agricultural community.

Wrestlingworth Village c1960 W302002 These two opposing views of the High Street have changed little since 1960.

Biggleswade, Market Square c1955 B93014 Much of the life of the town revolves around the Saturday influx to the weekly market. Pubs and cafés to cater for both thirst, and the occasional necessity to sit down to do business, surround Market Square. The 16th-century roof of the Market House, to the left of the picture, was preserved when road-widening operations took place in 1937.

Biggleswade, Market Place c1955 B93049
This must have been a quiet day in the Market Place, when it reverted to its more usual function of bus station and car park. The function of the cross supported on the pole in the middle foreground is not recorded, but logic suggests that it might be the site for a more ancient market cross. The 'Luncheons' sign on the building to the right and across the road from the Market House is the location of the Crown Hotel, the source of the Great Fire of Biggleswade in 1785.

Biggleswade, Market Square c1960 B93068

An active day on the benches in the Market Square, possibly just before opening time. Gale's radio and television store had a virtual monopoly for many years in Biggleswade. Many of the buildings surrounding the Square show evidence of ancient origins. In particular, the White Hart on the extreme right and the hipped-roofed building next to it have been on the site since the 16th century.

Biggleswade, Recreation Ground c1955 B93003

With an increasing number of community celebrations that have occurred in the second half of the 20th century - weddings, jubilees, and national anniversaries - Biggleswade's recreation ground has more than justified the investment in its facilities. An ornamental lake and a bandstand may seem to be anachronistic in a rural community, but the park has been at the heart of many successful events and family outings.

Index

The Francis Frith Collection Titles

www.francisfrith.co.uk

The Francis Frith Collection publishes over 100 new titles each year. A selection of those currently available is listed below. For latest catalogue please contact The Francis Frith Collection. **Town Books** 96 pages, approximately 75 photos. **County and Themed Books** 128 pages, approximately 135 photos (unless specified). All titles hardback with laminated case and jacket, except those indicated pb (paperback)

Accrington Old and New
Alderley Edge and Wilmslow
Amersham, Chesham and Rickmansworth
Andover
Around Abergavenny
Around Alton
Aylesbury
Barnstaple
Bedford
Bedfordshire
Berkshire Living Memories
Berkshire PA
Blackpool Pocket Album
Bognor Regis
Bournemouth
Bradford
Bridgend
Bridport
Brighton and Hove
Bristol
Buckinghamshire
Calne Living Memories
Camberley PA
Canterbury Cathedral
Cardiff Old and New
Chatham and the Medway Towns
Chelmsford
Chepstow Then and Now
Cheshire
Cheshire Living Memories
Chester
Chesterfield
Chigwell
Christchurch
Churches of East Cornwall
Clevedon
Clitheroe
Corby Living Memories
Cornish Coast
Cornwall Living Memories
Cotswold Living Memories
Cotswold Pocket Album
Coulsdon, Chipstead and Woodmanstern
County Durham
Cromer, Sheringham and Holt
Dartmoor Pocket Album
Derby
Derbyshire
Derbyshire Living Memories
Devon
Devon Churches
Dorchester

Dorset Coast PA
Dorset Living Memories
Dorset Villages
Down the Dart
Down the Severn
Down the Thames
Dunmow, Thaxted and Finchingfield
Durham
East Anglia PA
East Devon
East Grinstead
Edinburgh
Ely and The Fens
Essex PA
Essex Second Selection
Essex: The London Boroughs
Exeter
Exmoor
Falmouth
Farnborough, Fleet and Aldershot
Folkestone
Frome
Furness and Cartmel Peninsulas
Glamorgan
Glasgow
Glastonbury
Gloucester
Gloucestershire
Greater Manchester
Guildford
Hailsham
Hampshire
Harrogate
Hastings and Bexhill
Haywards Heath Living Memories
Heads of the Valleys
Heart of Lancashire PA
Helston
Herefordshire
Horsham
Humberside PA
Huntingdon, St Neots and St Ives
Hythe, Romney Marsh and Ashford
Ilfracombe
Ipswich PA
Isle of Wight
Isle of Wight Living Memories
King's Lynn
Kingston upon Thames
Lake District PA
Lancashire Living Memories
Lancashire Villages

Available from your local bookshop or from the publisher

The Francis Frith Collection Titles (continued)

Lancaster, Morecombe and Heysham Pocket Album
Leeds PA
Leicester
Leicestershire
Lincolnshire Living Memoires
Lincolnshire Pocket Album
Liverpool and Merseyside
London PA
Ludlow
Maidenhead
Maidstone
Malmesbury
Manchester PA
Marlborough
Matlock
Merseyside Living Memories
Nantwich and Crewe
New Forest
Newbury Living Memories
Newquay to St Ives
North Devon Living Memories
North London
North Wales
North Yorkshire
Northamptonshire
Northumberland
Northwich
Nottingham
Nottinghamshire PA
Oakham
Odiham Then and Now
Oxford Pocket Album
Oxfordshire
Padstow
Pembrokeshire
Penzance
Petersfield Then and Now
Plymouth
Poole and Sandbanks
Preston PA
Ramsgate Old and New
Reading Pocket Album
Redditch Living Memories
Redhill to Reigate
Rhondda Valley Living Mems
Richmond
Ringwood
Rochdale
Romford PA
Salisbury PA
Scotland
Scottish Castles
Sevenoaks and Tonbridge
Sheffield and South Yorkshire PA
Shropshire
Somerset
South Devon Coast
South Devon Living Memories
South East London
Southampton PA
Southend PA

Southport
Southwold to Aldeburgh
Stourbridge Living Memories
Stratford upon Avon
Stroud
Suffolk
Suffolk PA
Surrey Living Memories
Sussex
Sutton
Swanage and Purbeck
Swansea Pocket Album
Swindon Living Memories
Taunton
Teignmouth
Tenby and Saundersfoot
Tiverton
Torbay
Truro
Uppingham
Villages of Kent
Villages of Surrey
Villages of Sussex PA
Wakefield and the Five Towns Living Memories
Warrington
Warwick
Warwickshire PA
Wellingborough Living Memories
Wells
Welsh Castles
West Midlands PA
West Wiltshire Towns
West Yorkshire
Weston-super-Mare
Weymouth
Widnes and Runcorn
Wiltshire Churches
Wiltshire Living memories
Wiltshire PA
Wimborne
Winchester PA
Windermere
Windsor
Wirral
Wokingham and Bracknell
Woodbridge
Worcester
Worcestershire
Worcestershire Living Memories
Wyre Forest
York PA
Yorkshire
Yorkshire Coastal Memories
Yorkshire Dales
Yorkshire Revisited

See Frith books on the internet at www.francisfrith.co.uk

Frith Products & Services

Francis Frith would doubtless be pleased to know that the pioneering publishing venture he started in 1860 still continues today. Over a hundred and forty years later, The Francis Frith Collection continues in the same innovative tradition and is now one of the foremost publishers of vintage photographs in the world. Some of the current activities include:

Interior Decoration

Today Frith's photographs can be seen framed and as giant wall murals in thousands of pubs, restaurants, hotels, banks, retail stores and other public buildings throughout the country. In every case they enhance the unique local atmosphere of the places they depict and provide reminders of gentler days in an increasingly busy and frenetic world.

Product Promotions

Frith products are used by many major companies to promote the sales of their own products or to reinforce their own history and heritage. Frith promotions have been used by Hovis bread, Courage beers, Scots Porage Oats, Colman's mustard, Cadbury's foods, Mellow Birds coffee, Dunhill pipe tobacco, Guinness, and Bulmer's Cider.

Genealogy and Family History

As the interest in family history and roots grows world-wide, more and more people are turning to Frith's photographs of Great Britain for images of the towns, villages and streets where their ancestors lived; and, of course, photographs of the churches and chapels where their ancestors were christened, married and buried are an essential part of every genealogy tree and family album.

Frith Products

All Frith photographs are available Framed or just as Mounted Prints and Posters (size 23 x 16 inches). These may be ordered from the address below. From time to time other products - Address Books, Calendars, Table Mats, etc - are available.

The Internet

Already ninety thousand Frith photographs can be viewed and purchased on the internet through the Frith websites and a myriad of partner sites.

For more detailed information on Frith companies and products, look at these sites:

www.francisfrith.co.uk
www.francisfrith.com
(for North American visitors)

See the complete list of Frith Books at:

www.francisfrith.co.uk

This web site is regularly updated with the latest list of publications from The Francis Frith Collection. If you wish to buy books relating to another part of the country that your local bookshop does not stock, you may purchase on-line.

For further information, trade, or author enquiries please contact us at the address below:
The Francis Frith Collection, Frith's Barn, Teffont, Salisbury, Wiltshire, England SP3 5QP.
Tel: +44 (0)1722 716 376 Fax: +44 (0)1722 716 881 Email: sales@francisfrith.co.uk

See Frith books on the internet at www.francisfrith.co.uk

FREE PRINT OF YOUR CHOICE

Mounted Print
Overall size 14 x 11 inches (355 x 280mm)

Choose any Frith photograph in this book.
Simply complete the Voucher opposite and
return it with your remittance for £2.25 (to cover
postage and handling) and we will print the
photograph of your choice in SEPIA (size 11 x 8
inches) and supply it in a cream mount with a
burgundy rule line (overall size 14 x 11 inches).
Please note: **photographs with a reference
number starting with a "Z" are not Frith
photographs and cannot be supplied under
this offer.**
Offer valid for delivery to one UK address only.

PLUS: **Order additional Mounted Prints
at HALF PRICE - £7.49 each** (normally £14.99)
If you would like to order more Frith prints from
this book, possibly as gifts for friends and family,
you can buy them at half price (with no
additional postage and handling costs).

PLUS: **Have your Mounted Prints framed**
For an extra £14.95 per print you can have your
mounted print(s) framed in an elegant polished
wood and gilt moulding, overall size 16 x
13 inches (no additional postage and handling
required).

IMPORTANT!

**These special prices are only available if you use
this form to order. You must use the ORIGINAL
VOUCHER on this page (no copies permitted). We
can only despatch to one UK address. This offer
cannot be combined with any other offer.**

Send completed Voucher form to:
**The Francis Frith Collection, Frith's Barn,
Teffont, Salisbury, Wiltshire SP3 5QP**

CHOOSE A PHOTOGRAPH FROM THIS BOOK

Voucher for **FREE** and *Reduced Price Frith Prints*

*Please do not photocopy this voucher. Only the original is valid,
so please fill it in, cut it out and return it to us with your order.*

Picture ref no	Page no	Qty	Mounted @ £7.49	Framed + £14.95	Total Cost £
		1	Free of charge*	£	£
			£7.49	£	£
			£7.49	£	£
			£7.49	£	£
			£7.49	£	£
			£7.49	£	£

*Please allow 28 days
for delivery.
Offer available to one
UK address only*

* Post & handling	£2.25
Total Order Cost	£

Title of this book . . . .

I enclose a cheque/postal order for £ . . . .

made payable to 'The Francis Frith Collection'

OR please debit my Mastercard / Visa / Maestro card,
details below

Card Number

Issue No (Maestro only)   Valid from (Maestro)

Expires   Signature

Name Mr/Mrs/Ms . . . .
Address . . . .
. . . .
. . . .
. . . . Postcode . . . .
Daytime Tel No . . . .
Email . . . .

ISBN 1-84589-251-8   Valid to 31/12/08

Free Print – see overleaf

Would you like to find out more about Francis Frith?

We have recently recruited some entertaining speakers who are happy to visit local groups, clubs and societies to give an illustrated talk documenting Frith's travels and photographs. If you are a member of such a group and are interested in hosting a presentation, we would love to hear from you.

Our speakers bring with them a small selection of our local town and county books, together with sample prints. They are happy to take orders. A small proportion of the order value is donated to the group who have hosted the presentation. The talks are therefore an excellent way of fundraising for small groups and societies.

Can you help us with information about any of the Frith photographs in this book?

We are gradually compiling an historical record for each of the photographs in the Frith archive. It is always fascinating to find out the names of the people shown in the pictures, as well as insights into the shops, buildings and other features depicted.

If you recognize anyone in the photographs in this book, or if you have information not already included in the author's caption, do let us know. We would love to hear from you, and will try to publish it in future books or articles.

Our production team

Frith books are produced by a small dedicated team at offices in the converted Grade II listed 18th-century barn at Teffont near Salisbury, illustrated above. Most have worked with The Francis Frith Collection for many years. All have in common one quality: they have a passion for The Francis Frith Collection. The team is constantly expanding, but currently includes:

Andrew Alsop, Paul Baron, Jason Buck, John Buck, Heather Crisp, David Davies, Natalie Davis, Louis du Mont, Isobel Hall, Chris Hardwick, Lucy Hart, Julian Hight, Peter Horne, James Kinnear, Karen Kinnear, Tina Leary, Stuart Login, Sue Molloy, Miles Murray, Sarah Roberts, Kate Rotondetto, Dean Scource, Eliza Sackett, Terence Sackett, Sandra Sampson, Adrian Sanders, Sandra Sanger, Julia Skinner, Lewis Taylor, Shelley Tolcher, Lorraine Tuck, Miranda Tunnicliffe, Will Tunnicliffe, David Turner and Ricky Williams.